THE 7 SECRETS OF HIGHLY SUCCESSFUL PROPERTY INVESTORS

Your straight forward guide to building your own property portfolio

The 7 Secrets of Highly Successful PropertyInvestors

First Published in 2018 by Get More Pty Ltd
38 Winmalee Drive Glen Waverely Vic 3150
GetMore.com.au

A catalogue record for this
book is available from the
National Library of Australia

NATIONAL
LIBRARY
OF AUSTRALIA

ISBN: 978-0-994-170231 (pbk)
ISBN: 978-0-994-170248 (ebook)

Disclaimer:
The material in this publication is of the nature of general comment only, and does not represent professional advice. It is not intended to provide specific guidance for particular circumstance and it should not be relied on as the basis for any decision to take action or not take action on any matter which covers. Readers should obtain professional advice where appropriate, before making any such a decision. To the maximum extent permitted by law, the author and publisher disclaim all responsibility and liability to any person, arising directly or indirectly from any person taking or not taking action based on information in this publication

THE 7 SECRETS OF HIGHLY SUCCESSFUL PROPERTY INVESTORS

Your straight forward guide to building your own property portfolio

UWE JACOBS

ABOUT UWE JACOBS

Uwe Jacobs is the founding director of Property Friends and the author of the book The 7 Secrets of Highly Successful Property Investors. In the last decade alone, he has helped upwards of 325 clients amass property investments with a contract value of over AUD$135,000,000.

Uwe Jacobs has thirteen years worth of experience as a full-time property investor. When he founded the Property Friends system, his key aim was to provide his clients with residential real estate investment options that would help them realise financial independence. Many of his clients have gone on to achieve this and much more.

The Property Friends System is low risk, predictable and, most importantly, duplicable. Over the past 13 years, Uwe Jacobs and his team have helped create several net assets property millionaires.

His clientele extends from business owners and CEOs to mum and dad investors. All of them recommend his advice highly and continue to rave about their experience. Uwe Jacobs continues to suggest projects for his clients with one unique benchmark in mind: only what is good enough or Uwe and Ulla themselves, is good enough to discuss with their clients.

www.propertyfriends.com.au
Tel. +61 (0)3 9758 5331
info@propertyfriends.com.au

DEDICATION

For Ulla, Jessica and Christine
The best support crew ever

CONTENTS

INTRODUCTION

The Road to Success

Property Friends started almost by accident. Around 2005, Neil and Lynn McNabb approached me to help them buy an investment property like one my wife Ulla and I were planning to buy in Cairns. They had seen how we had been successful in buying properties which had impressive capital growth and above- average rental yields. Other people had also noted our achievements, so by the time we departed, three other investors had approached us in the same way.

We bought five properties on that trip and our friends were delighted with the results of the purchases we arranged on their behalf. They told their friends about what Ulla and I had gained for them ... and Property Friends was born.

We now have a network of people all over Australia and overseas who are buying investment properties, building their portfolios and reaping the lifestyle rewards that come with being in control of their financial futures.

I spent 25 years in the corporate world, running in the "rat race" at full speed, controlling major infrastructure projects, commercially managing billion dollar contracts and working around the clock to deliver results for someone else. I knew there had to be a better way.

Ulla and I had been investing in property the traditional way - buying, holding and waiting for values to go up. Our portfolio was negatively geared and the interest payments were choking us financially and emotionally. We wanted to build wealth for our future and for our two daughters, but we had to find an alternative method that would deliver a balance of capital growth and rental income in a way that was sustainable for the long-term, without the risk and stress we were under.

> ‘Some members of Property Friends
> have gained as much as $150,000 in
> equity within 12 months ... Others have
> built portfolios with net assets
> of more than $1 million.’

Better, safer, stronger investments

The Property Friends strategy is explained fully in later chapters, but suffice to say, we focus on new house and land packages in strategically selected parts of Australia that match our criteria focused on long-term capital growth, strong rental yield and Hassle-free investment.

We have developed a proven system that works for investors to buy quality properties at wholesale prices in the best locations, invariably before they are put on the market for sale.

Generally, Property Friends who buy a property valued at about $500,000 can expect to make at least $25,000 in group buying savings and capital gain before their first tenants move in. At best, some members of Property Friends have gained as much as $150,000 in equity within 12 months.

Refer to the Property Friends CD Real Estate Secrets Revealed (https://goo.gl/H3NQJp).

Others who have been with us a number of years have built portfolios with net assets of more than $1 million (i.e. the value of their properties is more than $1 million greater than their total loans).

Property Friends investors work as a team to secure group deals that guarantee savings when they buy and generate capital growth within the first years of their investment. Each investor signs individual contracts so no-one shares responsibility of any kind with anyone else, and every transaction and every cost is completely transparent.

Ulla and I manage every step of the process as though we were investing ourselves because often we are also investors in the same type of property in the same location at the same time. We put our money where our mouth is and guarantee that the saving and/or equity gain on completion of your property will be at least the value of our fee or we will give you a 100 per cent refund.

A proven track record

We do all the research and give you the road map to success, but we also insist that you do your own due diligence. After all, it's your money that you are spending. After arranging investments in more than 325 properties for members of Property Friends and ourselves since 2005, we have fine-tuned our methods so that every property purchase has predictable results. We pretty much know, before we put a dollar on the table, what the outcome of the transaction will be a year down the track.

We have a firm understanding of how each investment is likely to perform over five years, 10 years and longer because we painstakingly research areas before we visit them. We regularly travel all over Australia to gain first-hand knowledge of the areas in which Property Friends invest. We stay in the area, get to know people in the real estate and building industries and cross- reference our information with those who are working there to ensure each investment produces results.

Refer to the Property Friends CD Real Estate Secrets Revealed (https://goo.gl/H3NQJp).

Over the years we have established working relationships with builders, property developers, estate agents, quantity surveyors, valuers and all the consultants who are necessary for profitable property investment. We bring group buying power to earn savings for Property Friends and they earn multiple customers simultaneously.

Everyone wins

The Property Friends system is a win-win-win-win. Property Friends investors win because they buy quality properties under market value by buying as a group at wholesale, not retail, prices. The developers of the land win because the Property Friends Team buys five or 10 blocks simultaneously which accelerates their subdivision. The builders of our properties win because they get several houses to build at once which boosts their bottom line and Ulla and I win because we gain a fee for service - and a new friend.

Property Friends stay in touch with each other. Apart from the individual mentoring for all members, we have regular meetings where people in the team come together to hear about latest developments, new initiatives, movements in the market and learn from each other through shared experiences. We frequently host free webinars.

Check our website for details:
www.propertyfriends.com.au

Ulla and I started with $17,500. We now control a property portfolio worth several million. And it is a growth portfolio. Our properties pay us, not the other way around. This gives us the lifestyle choices we could only dream about when I was running on the corporate treadmill. Our goal was to be financially free and we are proud to have reached our objective.

But everyone's different and some people want only one or two investment properties to give them a little more cash flow and ease their financial pressures. Others want to build the biggest portfolio they can in the shortest time possible to replace their income and provide for their retirement.

Members of Property Friends are aged from 24 to 84. They have different goals but use the same method to achieve them. They have different attitudes to risk and debt and all can be accommodated within the Property Friends system. You are in the driver's seat. Our role is to help you get to where you want to go.

Chapter highlights

- Property Friends specialises in new house and land packages in strategically selected parts of Australia that achieve a balance of long-term capital growth and strong rental yield.

- Investors buy quality properties at wholesale prices in only the best locations, invariably before they are put on the market for sale.

- Working as a team to secure group deals, investors are expected to generate savings when they buy and generate capital growth within the first years of their investment.

- Each investor signs individual contracts so no-one shares responsibility of any kind with anyone else, and every transaction and every cost is completely transparent.

- Every property purchase has predictable results so that investors pretty much know, before they put a dollar on the table, what the outcome of the transaction will be.

- Property Friends stay in touch with each other through regular meetings about latest property developments, new initiatives, movements in the market and learn from each other through shared experiences.

YOU MUST HAVE A STRATEGY

Creating a Wealthy Future

People love the idea of a wealthy future, but they don't know where to start. From the outside it can look complex but once you get your head around it, it can be quite straight forward. One of the biggest dangers is that people don't have an underlying strategy and so they go with the current trend.

This is a recipe for disaster.

Like all worthwhile pursuits, an investment strategy sets the ground rules and keeps you focused while everything around you is changing. So, you need to have a look at some of the different options available to see what strategy will work best for your personal situation.

Investment is a simple word with a complex meaning. What's the best investment? Why? What are the risks? How does each type of investment differ? Which suits my personal circumstances, my goals, my risk profile and my future?

So many questions. But investment does not need to be as complicated as some people make it out to be. In basic terms, there are broadly three types of investment - cash, shares and property.

Cash

Cash in the bank is as safe as, well, cash in the bank. Provided the money is deposited with a solid, reputable bank like the big four in Australia (National Australia Bank, Commonwealth Bank, Westpac and ANZ), few people would have trouble sleeping at night if their money was invested in a bank term deposit.

The problem is that the returns on cash investments, while very secure, are generally substantially lower than the other two major asset classes. And once you allow for inflation and tax, the low- level profits from investing in cash are attractive to most people as only a short-term option while they consider a more productive decision to invest in shares, property or both.

Shares

Shares have recorded some fantastic gains - and horrific losses - over time. Some investors have made fortunes in the share market. Others have lost everything in the same way. Shares are regarded as a volatile investment because share prices can rise and fall sharply, sometimes within hours of major events or business announcements that affect industries and businesses.

People who invest in shares say there are principles which guide their decisions and protect against rapid falls in share prices.

They say that with research and discipline, the risks are manageable and the rewards worthwhile.

Shares are more liquid than property because they can be sold and bought quickly, unlike property which usually takes months to buy or sell. Investors who prefer shares to property say that they can sell a small parcel of their investment, but a property investor cannot sell one room of a property.

The big difference comes in leverage. Banks and financial institutions will generally lend up to 90+ per cent of a residential property's value, or more depending on circumstances, but generally up to a maximum of 60 per cent of the value of a portfolio of shares.

This means that people wanting to maximise the borrowing power of their investments can buy property of greater value than those buying shares if they have the same amount to invest.

Borrowing against shares also carries the risk of the lender requiring the borrower to pay more money into their loan account, or sell some shares, if the value of the shares decreases below a certain level. This is known as a margin call and it can require borrowers to find extra funds at short notice.

Property

Australians' love affair with the "great Australian dream" lives on. Aussies want property - the more of it the better. The stability and long-term value of bricks and mortar is etched in the minds of many investors.

More than 25 per cent of Australians rent and the nation's growing population will forever need accommodation, so the demand for residential property is expected to continue to be strong.

Like shares, property prices go up and down, but generally not as quickly or a sharply as share prices. Investors have confidence that the 1.6 million Australians who own investment property can't be wrong.

Buying property also brings tax advantages with income tax deductions for all expenses associated with investment property and depreciation can also be claimed against real estate buildings, fixtures and fittings.

Some investors prefer commercial property because the tenant generally pays all the out-goings and much of the maintenance costs, but vacancy periods can sometimes be far longer than what is normal for residential property.

And because everyone lives in a house or a unit, investors feel comfortable with the concept of buying a residential investment because it is something they understand.

Returns

Data over the past 30 years shows that Australian housing has produced average returns of more than 10 per cent a year when calculating capital growth and income. This is lower than returns for shares over the same period, but economics commentators suggest that property has one-third to half the risk of shares.

Average annual returns since 1982 of the asset classes are:

> Australian housing: 10.06 per cent
> Australian shares: 12.32 per cent Global shares: 10.15 per cent
> Australian Government bonds (10 year): 11.70 per cent Cash: 8.23 per cent
> Australian listed property trusts: 9.57 per cent

(Data source: Rismark International, a global funds management and advisory company).

Timeframe

For how long are you going to invest? A year or two, five or 10 years or longer?

Short term - up to 18 months

Most investments, especially property and shares, are long-term investments. The buying and selling costs mean that unless an investor buys exceptionally well they are unlikely to be able to return a significant profit with an investment term of less than 18 months.

This period can be sufficient to devise an investment strategy and set it on course. Research is the key to responsible investing and research takes time. Investors who don't have time to do research themselves at least need to research who they are going to trust to guide their investment strategy.

Medium term - 2 to 5 years

Share investors can reap double-digit growth within short periods, but this is by far the exception rather than the rule. Respected share investment advisors suggest investing in businesses that have long-term prospects of growth that will bring sustainable earnings and profits rather than trying to cherry pick the next "big thing" that will bring overnight results while running the risk of severe losses.

The best property investments are expected to double in value every seven years. Some take 10 years or more to double while others achieve such a gain in three or four years, depending on how the property market is performing.

Up to five years can be an adequate timeframe for carefully chosen property investments to generate sufficient growth that they can be sold for a substantial profit. But this leads to another question: Why are you selling?

The big bonus with property is that when it goes up in value so does your borrowing power. If an investor was thinking of selling to buy another property, they would be well advised to use the equity that has built up in their property, to buy another and keep both.

A brief look at history and a list of the world's richest people shows that many of the most financially successful people made their money by buying property and never selling.

Long term - 5 to 15 years

This is the territory of real investors keen to make serious profits to set themselves up financially for the future. Investors with a 15-year horizon are looking to create a nest egg that will give security for them and possibly their children as well.

How much is enough?

So how can you work out how long it will actually take to accumulate enough properties to provide for retirement at your desired level of income?

The simplest assessment is that if you want to retire on $60,000 a year, you will need unencumbered properties providing a net income which totals that amount, say three properties each producing $20,000 a year. Investors aiming for this would buy more than three during their working years and sell some at retirement to pay off the loans on those which will provide the on-going income.

Another rule of thumb is that you will need assets equal in value to your retirement income multiplied by 20, plus the value of your house and car. For example, if you want to retire on $50,000 a year in a house worth $700,000 and with a $40,000 car, you will need $50,000 x 20 = $1 million, plus $740,000 for the house and car, or a total of $1,740,000 in net assets.

If you already own your house and car without debt, you need $1 million in net assets to cover your annual retirement income of $50,000. Net assets equal the value of your properties after subtracting the total amount of the loans against them.

Several members of Property Friends have proved that with a disciplined approach and a clear strategy they have been able to buy a property every few years and set up their retirement plans over 10 years. Their earliest purchases have doubled in value and the properties bought later are well on their way to doing the same. Once all the properties have been retained through a seven to 10- year growth cycle they should each have doubled in value, turning the $1 million goal into reality.

'Investors who were buying new, four-bedroom properties off the plan last year for $441,000 have found they are worth well in excess of that figure by the time the houses have been completed this year. The first tenants are paying $520 a week, providing a gross rental yield of 6.15 per cent.'

YOU MUST HAVE A STRATEGY | 15

The power of time

The beauty of a long-term investment strategy is that the power of compound interest works wonders over time. As the value of the properties continues to grow, the debt on them remains the same or decreases, skyrocketing the net value of the assets - and throwing wide open the lifestyle choices that flow from buying the properties as early as possible.

It is a mathematical fact that even one or two properties bought over a 10-year period and allowed to grow naturally in value will be worth more in 20 years than perhaps double the number of properties bought over a shorter timeframe close to the end of the 20 years.

The secret to this outcome is not how much money you have to start with, how many properties you buy or even whether you buy the best investments, even though these factors are important. The real key to this element of the strategy is to buy as early as possible and allow inflation and capital growth to drive the value of your assets over time.

This proves another real estate truth: Time in the market is more valuable than timing when to buy. Investors who try to pick cycles in the market usually do not do better than others who buy as soon as they can. In every sense, time is your friend when you invest in property. The longer timeframe you have, or in other words, the earlier you begin, the better the result.

Success Story

David and Courtney Caruana

A self-funding portfolio

Aged 29, David Caruana is already in Australia's top one per cent of property investors. David and his wife Courtney own eight rental properties - and they are well on their way to building a multi-million dollar portfolio.

After only 10 years of investing in property their portfolio is so strong that they are now buying more properties with none of their own money. The equity that has been generated by the properties provides them with the funds to buy their next investment.

David, a crane driver, is humble about his success and admits that having two children has slowed his progress, but it's for his family's future that he embarked on his first investment as a 19-year-old.

At 24, he heard of Property Friends and in the past five years he has bought five properties arranged through Property Friends. Two are in Geraldton in Western Australia, and one in each of Cairns, Bowen and Rockhampton in Queensland.

The earliest of those purchases are moving towards doubling in value as most quality investments do over seven to 10 years. The property prices have been steadily increasing, as have the rents, and David said he follows the Property Friends recommendations of buying in areas that offer a mix of capital growth and rental yield in regions with solid infrastructure and economic diversity.

Figures from the Australian Tax Office show that of Australia's 1.6 million property investors, 73 per cent own only one property.

Eighteen per cent own two properties, 5.4 per cent own three properties, 2 per cent own four properties, less than one per cent own five properties and another less than 1 per cent (14,500 investors) own six or more properties.

Property strategy - growth versus income

There are generally two schools of thought about the best way to build wealth through property. One favours properties that grow in value - capital growth, or high growth properties. The other focuses on properties which produce an income in excess of what it costs to own them - cash flow positive properties, or high yield properties.

High growth

The backbone of the high growth strategy is to buy properties in prime locations, usually inner-city suburbs that are expected to grow in value more than any others. Property selection is based on historical data which shows the suburbs in which properties have a proven track record in producing the most outstanding price growth.

While most investors would love to own a portfolio of inner city terrace houses or art deco apartments, the obvious barrier is price.

Only the wealthiest can afford to buy such properties, and perhaps more importantly, pay to keep them. The price of the best high growth properties is such that once they are tenanted, many investors cannot afford to make the loan repayments, even after receiving the rent.

Unless an investor has a significant deposit, these properties are negatively geared, meaning their costs far exceed their income.

There is no doubt that high growth properties are great investments. After all, the escalating value of an asset is pivotal to its ability to generate wealth. But in today's market, the best high growth properties come with price tags of at least $700,000. And they produce low rental yields, of about 3 per cent, meaning that for every $1000 they cost, they produce an annual income of $30. This leads to a shortfall in cash, usually of thousands of dollars that the investor has to find and fund, in after tax dollars!

High yield

At the other end of the spectrum, some properties produce high yields, of 6 to 8 per cent, or more, with some of the best cash flow positive properties earning 15 per cent of their cost every year. And when interest rates are around 7 per cent a year, it's easy to see the attraction in high yield properties.

Investors who favour this type of property believe that cash flow is king because anything that earns more than it costs to hold has got to be good for the bottom line.

The downside to high yield properties is that they generally increase in value far less than high growth properties. So, while they pay an income, they sometimes contribute little else to wealth creation, so an investor usually needs to own a large number of them to replace their income.

Another difficulty with high yield properties is that they tend to be in remote areas, such as mining towns, or in locations that do not generate buyer demand.

The big advantage they have is that the best high yield properties will pay the investor handsomely. However, that income is often dependent on a single factor and if anything happens to that source of demand, such as a downturn in the mining industry, the income stream can, and does, diminish very quickly. Once the underlying demand for these properties is gone, they typically plummet in value quickly, creating a very fickle market.

However, there are investors who have bought properties in high yielding mining towns and they are earning $20,000 to $40,000 a year from a single property. Despite the favourable returns now, they need to watch these investments very closely because bad economic news in the region could lead to disaster.

A balance of growth and yield

It stands to reason that the best type of investment would be one which offers high growth and high yield. Unfortunately, most properties usually offer one or the other, not both.

At Property Friends, we take a balanced approach. Our business model is based on a healthy blend of growth and yield. Not the highest level of either category, because trying too hard for one usually discounts the other, but a sustainable mix of the two which comes from selecting properties that will grow solidly in value in locations that offer above-average yields due to a broad range of economic influences around them.

Refer to the Property Friends CD Property Strategies Revealed (https://goo.gl/RRmCui).

For example, Property Friends members have recently been buying new house and land packages in Rockhampton, on Queensland's coast, which offer annual yields of 6 to 7 per cent and projected capital growth based on previous sales results of 7 per cent a year. Additional uplift in values is expected due to Rockhampton's proximity to several major projects in the area.

Rockhampton produces growth and yield because it is a thriving regional centre and it has a diverse economic support base including a big beef industry, agriculture, mining in the hinterland and tourism.

Locations such as this are safe havens for investment because they do not rely on the success of one sector to keep the property market thriving. This means they will contribute to wealth creation through capital growth and they won't require large amounts of cash from investors to retain the properties, so property owners won't have to drain their lifestyle to pay for their investments.

'Once all the properties have been retained through a seven to 10-year growth cycle they have traditionally doubled in value, turning the $1 million goal into reality.'

An example that works

In Rockhampton, investors who were buying new, four-bedroom properties off the plan last year for $441,000 have found they are worth well in excess of that figure by the time the houses have been completed this year. The first tenants are paying $520 a week, providing a gross rental yield of 6.15 per cent, against a vacancy rate of 0.7 per cent, which shows that demand for rental properties is extremely high.

Cash flow calculations show that pre-tax, such a property will cost the investor $5888 a year, or $113 a week in the first year. But after tax deductions using the tax rate of 46.5 per cent, and depreciation calculations, the property is cash flow positive, earning $1185 a year, or $23 a week. In the second year, the property is cash flow positive by $2099 a year or $40 a week, after tax deductions and depreciation allowances.

If Rockhampton performs as expected according to historical data of previous sales results, the same property will be worth about $983,500 in 10 years. That will produce a profit, reflected in the asset growth or equity of about $533,000.

The following data shows a typical cash flow analysis of a Rockhampton property. It is an example and should be regarded as general information from the experience of Property Friends members and is not to be treated as financial advice.

Property Friends Pty Ltd - Melbourne

PROPERTY INVESTMENT ANALYSIS

Prepared for: Sample ONLY   02-Oct-2012
Consultant:
Property: Lot 364 Forrest Park, Rockhampton
Description: 700m2 land; 4x2x2 210m2 House by Bentley Builders

SUMMARY

Assumptions		Projected results over	10yrs
Property value	$500,000	Property value	$983,576
Initial investment	$1,000	Equity	$533,366
Gross rental yield	6.15%	After tax return/yr	282.37%
Net rental yield	4.90%	Net present value	$388,081
Cap. growth rate	7.00%	**IF SOLD**	
Inflation rate	4.00%	Selling costs & CGT	$166,751
Interest rate	6.00%	Equity	$366,615
Marginal tax rate	46.50%	After tax return/yr	282.26%

COMPUTER PROJECTIONS

Investment Analysis		Projections over 10 years				
End of year	2012	1yr	2yr	3yr	5yr	10yr
Property value	$500,000	535,000	572,450	612,522	701,276	983,576
Purchase costs	$19,265					
Investments	$1,000					
Loan amount	$450,210	450,210	450,210	450,210	450,210	450,210
Equity	$49,790	84,790	122,240	162,312	251,066	533,366
Capital growth rate	7.00%	7.00%	7.00%	7.00%	7.00%	7.00%
Inflation rate (CPI)	4.00%	4.00%	4.00%	4.00%	4.00%	4.00%
Gross rent/week	$520	26,499	27,559	28,662	31,000	37,717
Cash deductions						
Interest (IO)	6.00%	27,013	27,013	27,013	27,013	27,013
Rental expenses	19.88%	5,375	5,590	5,814	6,288	7,650
Pre-tax cash flow	**$-1,000**	-5,888	-5,043	-4,165	-2,300	3,050
Non-cash deductions						
Deprec of building	2.50%	5,925	5,925	5,925	5,925	5,925
Deprec of fittings	$20,000	3,208	4,202	2,906	1,496	439
Loan costs	$945	189	189	189	189	
Total deductions		41,710	42,919	41,846	40,911	41,027
Tax credit	46.50%	7,073	7,142	6,131	4,608	1,539
After tax cash flow	**$-1,000**	1,185	2,099	1,966	2,308	4,593
Rate of return (IRR)	282.37%	Your cost/(income) per week				
Pre-tax equivalent	527,80%	(23)	(40)	(38)	(44)	(88)

Disclaimer: Note that the computer projections listed above simply illustrate the outcome calculated from the input values and the assumptions contained in the model. Hence the figures can be varied as required and are in no way intended to be a guarantee of future performance. Although the information is provided in good faith, it is also given on the basis that no person using the information, in whole or in part, shall have any claim against Property Friends Pty Ltd - Melbourne.

Property investment is a great way to earn money, either through direct income or growth in asset values. It can set you free. But it shouldn't be done in a way that means you have to put your life on hold for 10 years. It shouldn't be such a financial burden that you can't go on holidays or enjoy a few treats because you're contributing to an investment strategy that aims to give you those same benefits later in life.

Investing in property is a way of taking control of your financial destiny and it is vital to do that in today's changing world where the size of the ageing population is likely to prevent future governments from providing a favourable pension system. As a mentor once said to me, "If it is to be, it's up to me", and I agree with him.

Many Baby Boomers will find they have to cater for their own retirement or else they will end up like the 80 per cent of Australian retirees on an income of less than $21,000 a year.

Success Story

Stress-free money making

Sara Shaw's first investment arranged by Property Friends skyrocketed in value by more than 80 per cent in two years.

It was not only an outstanding investment, but it also threw Sara a lifeline when she needed it.

Sara, a graphic designer, bought a three-bedroom house and land package in Geraldton in Western Australia for $254,000. Within a year it had grown in value to $350,000 and another year later it was worth $465,000.

Sara Shaw

"The land went up in value by $50,000 even before we built on it," Sara said.

"Unfortunately, I had bought another investment which wasn't so good before using Property Friends and I had to sell this one to make up the difference, but I was lucky I had it there," Sara said. Sara was not concerned about investing thousands of kilometres from where she was living.

"Uwe was on the ground and it was obvious he knew his stuff which gave me confidence, so I didn't feel I had to go to WA," she said.

"Uwe did all the work and Property Friends was very professional to deal with. Whenever I was wondering how things were progressing, they sent me an update before I asked.

"It was a very stress-free way of making great money. I only wish I had more available cash to do another one with them."

Chapter highlights

- Choose an investment strategy that suits your personal circumstances, goals, risk profile and future plans.

- Shares can be a volatile investment and property is generally more stable, but the big difference is in the leverage that banks will offer, making property a standout investment.

- Investors have confidence that the 1.6 million Australians who own investment property can't be wrong.

- The big bonus with property is that when it goes up in value so does an investor's borrowing power. Anyone thinking of selling to buy another property would be well advised to use the equity that has built up in their property to buy another and keep both.

- A brief look at history and a list of the world's richest people shows that many of the most financially successful people made their money by buying property and never selling.

- Investors with a 15-year horizon can create a nest egg that will give security for them and possibly their children as well.

- The beauty of a long-term investment strategy is that the power of compound interest works wonders over time. As the value of the properties continues to grow, the debt on them remains the same or decreases, skyrocketing the net value of the assets.

- The secret is not how much money you have to start with, how many properties you buy or even whether you buy the best investments. The real key is to buy as early as possible and allow inflation and capital growth to drive the value of your assets over time.

- Time in the market is more valuable than timing when to buy.

- The Property Friends business model is based on a healthy blend of growth and yield which comes from selecting properties that will grow solidly in value in locations that offer above-average yields due to a broad range of economic influences around them. The properties do not require large amounts of cash from investors, so owners don't have to drain their lifestyle to pay for their investments.

GET YOUR ASSET SELECTION RIGHT

How to get RichSafely

The time for action has come. You've researched the property market and satisfied yourself that there is money to be made by investing in property. You have assessed your finances and know you can buy. You've read investment books and magazines and feel you have the confidence to take the plunge. But which type of property will you buy? Where? And how will you know that your investment is safe and that it will meet your objectives?

There are many ways of investing in property, and done properly, each of them can be successful, with varying levels of risk and reward. Select which type of asset will be the best investment for you will depend on your goals, your timeframe, your attitude to risk and debt and a range of other factors.

There are advantages and disadvantages with each type of property investment. Here is a summary of the major options.

Established property - buy and hold

Most investors buy houses or units and rent them to tenants to help pay the mortgage. They usually buy close to where they live because they feel comfortable investing in an area they know and where they can keep an eye on their investment. They find a local property manager to manage the property and adopt a 'buy, rent and pray' approach, hoping the investment will be hassle-free and deliver them a windfall in years to come.

Often, with established properties, the negative gearing associated with the investment prevents (or restricts) the investor from building a portfolio. And when things get tough, it is easy to lose focus on what you have set out to achieve. This is why, of the 1.6 million property investors in Australia, a whopping 73 per cent own only one property and fail to build a portfolio.

Those who accumulate several properties leverage from one property to the next as the value of their existing properties increases. Their ability to do this is governed by the quality of the investments they buy, the rate at which they grow in value and the income they earn.

Too often, the balance between expenses and income becomes too difficult to juggle and when the going gets tough the portfolio building grinds to a halt.

Many 'buy and hold' property owners become investors almost by accident when they inherit the family home. This type of investor is less likely to cast a critical eye over the property to ensure it meets their needs as an investment.

Similarly, there is some reluctance to assess their goals and discover how this property may, or may not, help them reach those goals. They have a "hands off" attitude that does nothing to enhance the financial possibilities that could be achieved if they were more proactive.

It is amazing that many people work extremely hard for their money, but don't make their money or assets work just as hard for them.

Maintenance is often a big issue, especially with older properties, that can cause financial and emotional strain.

Renovation

Television property makeover shows have a lot to answer for. What looks so cheap and easy on TV is not usually so simple in reality, unless you are a tradesman or know some who will do you favours.

Cost blow-outs on renovation jobs are common, unless you are experienced. If you budget on tradesmen doing the work, a renovation can be very expensive. If you do much of the work yourself, the job can be tough, time-consuming and stressful, especially if your mortgage commitments require you to work to a strict deadline.

Time is critical: the longer it takes you to prepare the property, the longer the property is sitting there without earning a rental income.

With solid project management skills, financial knowledge and a flair for renovation on a budget, property renovation can be a sound investment strategy.

The results of renovation work can be very satisfying and financially rewarding, but the journey to reach that point can be painful. Most successful renovators say they learnt a lot on their first couple of projects and that experience guided them to the success they enjoyed later.

Property development

This is property investment on steroids. Take all the potential pitfalls of property investment and add in the challenges presented by town planning regulations, local council politics, involvement of resident action groups and the reluctance of banks to finance anything but the most profitable projects and you have part of the picture of property development.

Transforming an old house on a large block into a two or three unit development has been a golden goose for many builders, but fewer are in this market now than they were even a few years ago.

Property development is not for the faint-hearted. Only the experienced, well-financed operators with established industry relationships survive.

Land banking

To anyone with enough money, land banking sounds like a great idea. Given that property almost always goes up in value over time, why not buy a chunk of land in a great spot, sit on it, and wait for it to bring you wealth?

The obvious downfall of this strategy is that one needs substantial available cash to be able to buy and hold land, which is often vacant and not producing income, for a long time. And even if you did have the money, wouldn't you be better applying it to a more active wealth-creation strategy?

Off-shore purchases

With the crash of the American economy in recent years, news of the global financial crisis erupting from the mortgage belts of the USA and the spike in the value of the Australian dollar, investors have been buying American real estate at unbelievably low prices.

Properties have been sold for as little as a few thousand dollars, and when rented have produced yields up to 30 per cent a year. A few investors have done very well, but some have been throwing good money after bad.

As is always the case in real estate, location is vital. And if properties are selling for a fraction of their value, there's always a reason for that. There are also numerous hurdles that Australian investors must jump over to buy in the United States and property laws there are obviously different.

For example, property management is not regulated like it is in Australia, and there have been many stories of American "managers" handling investors' rental income in creative ways.

Exchange rates and foreign legislation are two other risks which are completely beyond the control of the investor, which is why some people consider offshore investing to be similar to gambling.

The lesson here is that nothing can take the place of detailed research.

Rent to buy

There is a niche property market in Australia involving 'wraps'. In a nutshell, a wrap is a contract that allows a tenant to lease a property for above-average rent on the condition that they will eventually be able to buy the property from the landlord. The system is based on the property owner gaining an exceptionally high yield in the early years of the contract in return for the tenant being able to own the property later.

This scheme has never taken off because too many property owners and tenants see shortcomings with it. With that said, it has worked well for some investors, allowing them to gain higher than expected income. It can be just as advantageous for tenants who might not otherwise have been able to secure a property of their own.

Commercial property

Investors in commercial property are often graduates from residential property or business people who have leased commercial premises, seen the advantages of being a landlord, and bought their own commercial property.

Many in this sector do not invest in residential property because they prefer the advantages of commercial property. Commercial tenants usually pay most, if not all, of the property's outgoing expenses, tenants are often locked in to rent increases in long-term tenancy contracts and tenants usually pay much of the maintenance costs because they want their businesses to operate in attractive, well-functioning buildings.

The downside is that commercial properties are generally more expensive than residential properties and vacancy periods can be much longer, meaning that investors need to be financially strong. Rental yields are often high and capital growth low but with properties that have high yields and high growth, the purchase price is extreme. With commercial properties that are purpose-built, vacancy periods can be extreme once the initial tenant vacates.

'Of the 1.6 million property investors in Australia, 73 per cent of them own only one property and fail to build a portfolio.'

House and Land Packages

After detailed assessment and trial and error in many of the sectors already described, Property Friends has been established with a business model focused purely on house and land packages. Why? Because that's where we believe investors get the biggest bang for their buck. In other words, new house and land packages - when bought using Property Friends methods - give the best balance of yield, growth and security of any sector in the property market.

Refer to the Property Friends CD Property Strategies Revealed (*https://goo.gl/RRmCui*).

Investors can chase high yield in mining towns and earn big incomes. But what happens if the mine in that town closes? Others can secure fantastic capital growth with inner city properties, but how much does it cost out of the investor's pocket every week to pay the mortgage?

With our house and land packages, all the costs and the income are known before anyone puts a dollar on the table or signs anything. This is vitally important. Every investor knows what the outcome of their investment is likely to be before they commit to the process. They have the experience of others who have gone before them, using the same tried and tested methods, to show that the Property Friends system works.

Buying a house and land package the Property Friends way is not the same as buying a house and land package in any new housing development from any builder or developer. Like the advertising slogan of seafood company John West, "It's the tuna John West rejects that makes John West the best", the volume of similar house and land packages that Property Friends ignores is part of the reason why the ones the company selects are successful and profitable.

Property Friends travels extensively all over Australia to find the best cities in which to buy properties, and once we find the best locations we select the best new housing developments in those cities and we then choose the best individual house sites within those estates.

We always sprinkle our houses around the estate so we can use one or two floor plans, with different facades and colours, to make them look individually attractive. This also protects the integrity of the estate, by avoiding a street where all the houses look like rental properties.

Next, we select the best house design suited to each site, depending on its orientation and other factors, and we incorporate design features into each house to make it the most attractive and user friendly it can be for the price. For example, we often take out walk-in robes and replace them with study areas because that brings more rent which is ultimately what we're seeking as investors.

We also plan the design according to its location. In Victoria, houses with north-facing outdoor entertaining patios are popular but in Queensland a similar property would be better served by installing air conditioning.

Research, research, research

We explore a range of research tools, some of which are free and some to which we subscribe, to select three to five areas a year on which we focus our attention. We examine property price changes over historical periods and recent years, we look at rental prices and their movements over time and we study a vast range of factors including population and age data, income, job classifications of residents, unemployment and educational standards, to name a few.

We do a major study of the economic background of the area. Why is it a growing region? What are the factors that will continue, or restrict, its continued development? Are new residents being attracted to the city and why? What are the economic drivers of the region? Does it have a diversity of industries which support the area?

This is very important, because a city that has multiple support bases will always underpin a long-term investment as it has various sectors which will contribute to its future if one industry goes through a rough period.

Are there major educational institutions in the city? Are job prospects growing? How broad is planned future development? Are major companies investing in the area? What is causing them to do so? Are government initiatives driving growth? What does State and Federal Government policy say about the future of the city?

What new infrastructure such as freeways and train stations are planned? When?

These are just some of the questions to which we gain answers before we drill down into deciding whether a location is suitable for us to recommend buying property there.

After we are satisfied that a city has the economic foundations, diversity and growth to support long-term investment, we immerse ourselves in the real estate and building industries of the city. We visit locations several times, even for a week at a time, at different times of the year so we see the city at its worst and best. We go at quiet and busy times of the year to see how the city works and feel how vibrant it is or is not.

Expert help for top results

We talk to real estate agents, builders and developers and cross- reference information from each of them with the others. When the same names continue to be presented as reliable, honest and efficient professionals, we begin to narrow our focus on the best operators for our jobs.

As a licensed real estate agent in Victoria and Queensland, I understand how the profession works and the tricks agents use in negotiation.

We look at all the new land for sale and coming up for sale in the near and distant future. Often we are returning to a city because we have been buying property there in the past and we come back to introduce new buyers to new opportunities, which we knew would be coming up. Sometimes we will do nothing initially but return a year or two later to select the best properties when they are available.

In this way, we are able to take advantage of many properties before they are available publicly on the open market. We often buy "off market" land because we had ear-marked it, even when it existed only on draft subdivision plans, before any formal documents had been presented to the local council for approval.

Throughout this process we are building relationships with land developers, builders and estate agents that are important to our continued success. The contacts we establish appreciate that we are important to them because Property Friends brings groups of buyers to do business with them, sometimes several times.

> '**With Property Friends house and land packages, all the costs and the income are known before anyone puts a dollar on the table or signs anything.**'

Wholesale / Group buying power

Usually Property Friends investors buy five to 10 house and land packages in the selected development. The power of buying as a group ensures we get the best possible deals on everything, from the amount of deposit that has to be paid, until the finishing touches of the completed property.

One of the keys to the success of the Property Friends system is that we buy a retail product at wholesale prices. Many property investment experts say that the best investors make a profit when they buy, not when they sell. This is exactly what we do, and have proven to do so over a long period of investing in several states of Australia.

Generally, an investor buying a property supported by Property Friends, will make a minimum of $25,000 in equity and group buying savings between the time they sign the purchase contract and when the first tenants arrive less than 12 months later.

On our best deals, when the property market has been hot, some investors have enjoyed capital gains of $150,000 while the house was constructed. At worst, during the peak of the Global Financial Crisis when price growth was swallowed by economic turmoil, investors broke even. What they paid for their property was its market value when the tenants moved in.

We charge an overhead recovery fee for providing the Property Friends service to you. This involves a one-on-one assessment with you of what you want to achieve through your investment, individual mentoring with you about which property is best for you according to your risk profile and your selection of the property.

We do all the ground work and can assist in the administration to ensure your property is built on time according to budget. We oversee the drawing up of contracts to ensure they are favourable to Property Friends investors and our standing by your side on these matters ensures that houses do not incur extra hidden costs during construction.

We encourage you to use your own advisers such as finance brokers, solicitors and insurance agents, but we have established contacts with all the necessary consultants if you choose to use them.

It is important to use some consultants from the state in which we are buying. For example, it is recommended to use solicitors or conveyancers for purchases from the state in which the property is located because state laws differ, and they best know the laws in their own state.

When Property Friends investors buy a number of properties at once, we generally select two respected property management agencies in the city to negotiate rental agreements on behalf of the group. Invariably, we get the best deals available because the property managers see the arrival of new business in bulk and sharpen their pencils to win it.

This keeps the managers honest and ensures they perform at their best. If they don't, they run the risk of losing the business just as quickly as it arrived and forever being overlooked for future business which will often follow. This way, we not only get very favourable prices, but even better, we earn outstanding service.

Refer to the Property Friends CD Property Strategies Revealed (https://goo.gl/RRmCui).

Investors are independent with Property Friends support

As an investor using the Property Friends system, you sign the property purchase contract for the land and the construction contract for the house to be built. All contractual transactions are direct between you and the builder or land developer.

The role of Property Friends is to introduce the parties to each other and to represent the interests of Property Friends investors in negotiating the transactions to gain the benefits of buying as a group. We buy as a group, but each person does not share responsibility for their transaction with anyone else.

Ulla and I started building our property portfolio in exactly the same way we recommend to others through Property Friends. And we continue to do so. Of the five or 10 buyers in each development, Ulla and I are often one of the purchasers.

We buy at exactly the same price as all others in the group, in exactly the same location at the same time with the same builders constructing the same houses. We put our money where our mouth is because we know it works.

Property Friends is paid by you for the service we give. No other party or business or person pays anything to Property Friends.

There are no commission's payable for anything by anyone. The fee for service charged by Property Friends is completely transparent and separate from your contracts over the property. This is a refreshing difference to other operators in the market. Being independent of any "kickbacks" means Property Friends is free to choose and move or stay with only the best operators.

Once your investment is up and running, the involvement with Property Friends continues as much as you want it to. We have regular meetings, on-going education programs, newsletters and webinars to keep you up to date with new developments, movements in the property market and help you to interact with others in the group.

Building a portfolio, or not

Some Property Friends members choose to buy one or two properties. Others want to build a portfolio. There is no right or wrong way to go. It depends on what you want to achieve and how you want to go about doing it. The role of Property Friends is to open the door of opportunity to you and encourage you to step inside when it suits you, with our support and guidance.

Typically, Property Friends targets locations in cities which offer above-average capital growth and rental yields of at least 5 per cent. Since 2005 we have assisted investors to buy more than 350 house and land packages in Victoria, Queensland, Western Australia, Tasmania and the Northern Territory.

Join millionaire's row

Some of the investors who started with us at the beginning of Property Friends are already millionaires with the equity they have built in their portfolios beyond what the properties cost. Like everyone, they started with one property and saw that it was meeting their investment objectives, so they bought another and then another, repeating the same process.

One of the benefits of the Property Friends system is that properties earning at least 5 per cent yield provide solid income, enabling the investment to be repeated, especially when they are also achieving solid capital growth that improves borrowing power.

Big gains, low risk

Of all the ways of investing in property, buying house and land packages the way we do it offers the best reward at the lowest risk. We have a fixed price for the land and generally a fixed price for the house. We know what rents comparable properties are achieving and we know all the expenses. That represents a low risk profile for a relatively high return, when combined with our group buying power, ensures Property Friends investors always get a great deal.

We buy brand new homes which keeps maintenance costs down for years and attracts a broad group of tenants who love living in new homes. And we get maximum tax deductions through depreciation on the new building and fixtures which is an added bonus.

Adam Johnston

Forecasts bring big rewards

Property Friends has twice correctly forecast growth in sectors of the Australian residential property market for investor Adam Johnston.

First in Cairns in North Queensland and then in Geraldton in Western Australia, Property Friends accurately identified property growth markets before they boomed.

Adam followed the Property Friends recommendations and was rewarded with impressive capital growth of up to $100,000 in 18 months.

"They were on the money," Adam said. "They picked the right spot at the right time.

"It was easy from my end. I just paid the money and a house popped out the other end.

"I was too time-poor to go through the process and hassle of finding the right property.

"Agreeing to buy my first property through somebody I'd only spoken to over the phone was quite a leap of faith. In fact, I only met Uwe after buying my second. But from land to builders, solicitors, lenders, real estate agents, building inspectors and quantity surveyors, Uwe had all the bases covered, and everyone I have dealt with has really been on the ball," Adam said.

"My second property was vacant for all of half an hour as the prospective tenant was hassling me to get my bank to push the final settlement through so they could move in straight away.

"It is now returning 6.4 per cent and has increased in value at least $100,000 in the 18 months from when I put the first $500 down to construction complete."

Chapter highlights

- New house and land packages get the biggest bang for your buck at the lowest risk when bought using Property Friends methods. They give the best balance of yield, growth and security of any sector in the property market, because there is a fixed price for the land and usually a fixed price for the house. We know what rents comparable properties are achieving and we know all the expenses.

- Every Property Friends investor knows what the outcome of their investment is likely to be before they commit to it. They have the experience of others who have gone before them, using the same tried and tested methods, to show that the system works.

- Property Friends travels extensively all over Australia to find the best cities in which to buy properties, then selects the best new housing developments in those cities and the best individual house sites.

- Major research into the economy, infrastructure, employment, growth and historical data of a city is vital to determine the best investment locations.

- Property Friends often buys "off market" land after it has been ear- marked when it existed only on draft subdivision plans, before being presented to the local council for approval.

- Relationship building is vital to the Property Friends way of doing business because it retains valuable contacts and ensures efficiency, high quality and top service.

- Group buying power enables retail products to be bought at wholesale prices and ensures the best possible deals on everything from the amount of deposit that has to be paid, until the finishing touches of the completed property.

- Investors generally make a minimum of $25,000 in equity and group buying savings between the time they sign the purchase contract and when the first tenants arrive less than 12 months later.

- Investors sign the purchase contract for the land and the construction contract for the house directly with the builder or land developer. No-one shares responsibility for their transaction with anyone else.

- Investors pay Property Friends for the service they receive. No other party, business or person pays anything to Property Friends. There are no hidden commission's payable for anything by anyone.

- Brand new homes keep maintenance costs down for years and attract a broad group of tenants who love living in new homes. They also attract maximum tax deductions through depreciation.

USE LEVERAGE TO MAGNIFY YOUR RETURN.

The Power of Leverage

Archimedes said, "Give me a lever long enough and a fulcrum on which to place it, and I shall move the world."

Leverage is the power of doing one small thing and enabling a much larger shift. In terms of investing, it means investing a small amount but getting returns as if you had invested far more.

Let me explain in more detail.

Finance

If you could buy something valued at $1000 for $100 would you do it?

What if you knew that the $1000 was expected to grow to $2000 within a decade - and that you would still owe no more than $100 at that time?

And what if you were paid by someone who used it during those years and paid again by the Tax Office because the Government wants to encourage what you are doing?

Sound like a pretty good deal? Welcome to the world of property investment.

Most people who buy investment properties do so because they think it makes financial sense to use someone else's money to help them to become wealthy.

The power of leverage, like the advantage of time and the effect of compound interest, makes investing in property one of the world's greatest opportunities.

In no other way can investors multiply the value of what they own to the same extent than they can with property.

This is because banks and lending institutions love property. They know it holds its value over time and therefore they are happy to lend against it like nothing else on Earth.

Property generates income, but more importantly, it grows in value over the long term. A loan against property differs wildly from a loan against most other things because it is supported by the tangible asset of bricks and mortar, market demand and historical proof that it leads to wealth.

Indeed, debt against property is "good" debt because it is supported by assets which increase in value over time. Debt for consumables such as cars is "bad" debt because the value of the product underpinning the debt goes down immediately and irreversibly from the day the loan begins.

It is for these reasons that the link between property and finance is so important. Taken from a different perspective, finance can be viewed as the reason why property is such a popular investment. If it were not for the ability of property to gain the level of finance that it does, property would not be such an attractive investment.

Have you taken a look at the *Business Review Weekly* Rich List? Question: What is the common denominator among many of Australia's mega-wealthy? Answer: Property.

How have the super-rich accelerated their accumulation of wealth? By using finance to borrow against property to buy more property. They understand the power of leverage that allows them to invest a small amount to control an asset worth a large amount.

On a smaller scale, smart property investors do the same. They invest between 5 per cent and 20 per cent of their own money to control 100 per cent of an asset. They gain 100 per cent of the income and enjoy 100 per cent of the growth in the asset's value, but again, they contribute up to only 20 per cent of the property's purchase price.

In this way, investors have their money working for them as hard as possible. They maximise their borrowings to magnify the long-term gains from their investments.

That's why I call leverage the "holy cow" of property investment. Leverage allows investors to control assets worth far more than they can buy with their own money and to gain all the long-term advantages that flow from their investments. Combined with the benefits that come with owning property over time, leverage accelerates the growth in asset values that property can bring.

As a result, property is the most powerful investment vehicle, especially given its security and relative stability. Simply, property is the golden egg that leads to future prosperity, provided it is handled with respect and used responsibly.

But not everyone wants to borrow as much as the banks will allow them. Different people have varying risk profiles and their financial goals are also different. But the theory remains, that leverage through property, at any level, is a key to generating wealth.

In heady years gone by, property buyers could borrow up to 106 per cent of a property's value. This was dangerous, and it caused heartbreak for many who could not manage the repayments and became particularly unsavory when some properties against which the loans were made declined in value over the short term to below their purchase price.

Nowadays, the finance market for property investors has returned to a more sustainable level where banks will lend up to 80 per cent for standard residential loans without mortgage insurance, up to 95 per cent with mortgage insurance, and 65 to 70 per cent for residential development loans.

That suits responsible investors who like safe investments in proven areas of capital growth with above-average rental yields. It means their investments can stay on track to secure long-term advantages that create wealth.

And it means that figuratively speaking, you can still buy a $1000 asset with $100 of your own money.

'Property investors can invest between
5 per cent and 20 per cent of their own
money to control 100 per cent of an asset.'

Purchasing power

"Cheaper by the dozen", "buy in bulk and save" and "two for the price of one" are slogans that have been used forever by traders to generate sales. So why not repeat it back to them when you can be part of a group buying team?

That's what Property Friends does - and the savings flow to individual investors to the tune of thousands of dollars with every transaction.

Property Friends usually arranges the purchase of five to 10 house and land packages in an estate at once.

It never ceases to amaze me how the appeal of multiple buyers opens doors to savings and opportunities.

Refer to the Property Friends CDs Real Estate Secrets Revealed (*https://goo.gl/H3NQJp*) and Property Strategies Revealed (*https://goo.gl/RRmCui*).

Put simply, we use our group purchasing power to get a better deal. When we are negotiating to buy land for houses, we know the prices that single blocks are selling for and we ask for - and get - discounts because the vendor gains an advantage in trading several sites simultaneously.

In the early stages of a subdivision, one of the best stages in which to buy, the land developer often has to generate a certain number of sales before he can gain bank finance to carry out the site works of drainage, sewerage and road construction. A quick sale of a group of blocks can mean the difference between a quick start to the construction phase or costly delays, so developers are often keen to lower their prices a little if we can help their project.

Buying as a group also brings advantages in site selection. Being able to choose the best location in an estate, or the most favourable orientation of a block, can be a significant benefit when it comes to renting or selling.

For example, it might be an advantage to have the sun flowing into the living areas of a house in Victoria, but in Queensland it might be best to maximise the afternoon shade.

What's best for one area might not be the preferred option for another. But by buying early in an estate's development, with group buying power, Property Friends usually get ideal outcomes.

Group buying also brings savings when dealing with builders. They save money if they can build several houses at the same time in the same area, especially if they have similar floor plans and specifications. Like land developers, they are particularly keen to do deals, if they know that Property Friends is active in the area and is likely to bring them more clients in the future.

Group buying power also holds influence over tradesmen and suppliers. If any of them do not do the right thing by anyone in Property Friends, word soon spreads, and they risk losing multiple deals and tarnishing their name for future sales.

Similarly, property managers, insurance brokers, quantity surveyors, valuers and other professionals such as land surveyors and even soil testing companies look after Property Friends when they know we have a group of clients in their area.

Leverage from group buying is rarely maximised by property investors, but it is a significant advantage when used the Property Friends way.

'The power of leverage, like the advantage of time and the effect of compound interest, makes investing in property one of the world's greatest opportunities.'

Service providers

Not only does Property Friends get favourable prices, but we also get preferential treatment. Service standards are at their best since we have the clout to demand the best. We make it known that we expect efficient, reliable and professional service and invariably we get it from our service providers.

In rare cases where consultants or service providers let us down, we let them know that we are unhappy and ask them to improve immediately. If they can't, we politely move our business elsewhere. It works in our favour that small business people do their best to keep good clients, especially when there is the perceived risk of losing a group of them if they don't. And it ensures that Property Friends gain levels of service rarely seen elsewhere.

Success Story

Dion and Jacinta Cachia

Strength in numbers

When Dion and Jacinta Cachia travelled interstate to Townsville to inspect their new rental property, they were impressed with the quality of the finished product - and the determination of the builder to do the right thing by Property Friends.

They said it was immediately apparent that the builder wanted to do an excellent job, partly because he knew it was important for him to win other contracts from Property Friends members.

At one stage, there was a problem with some of the tiling, but the builder immediately arranged to fix it and contacted Property Friends with a solution, not a problem.

"The builder was into doing quality work to keep in with the group," Dion said. "He saw that we were one part of a bigger picture for him. "We felt there was a lot of protection in the strength of the group."

Dion said he believed the service they got from the builder and property manager was better than they would have received if they were operating alone and the quality and location of the house was better than they would have chosen independently.

"Trying to buy a property interstate is something we would probably never have done on our own and we probably would have made the mistake of picking something that wouldn't have given us the same result as we have now," Dion said.

The couple was so impressed with the outcome of their first investment property they quickly bought a second one arranged by Property Friends.

Chapter highlights

- Banks love property. They know it holds its value over time and they are happy to lend against it like nothing else on Earth. Therefore, investors can multiply the value of what they own through property, more than through any other class of assets.

- Debt against property is "good" debt because it is supported by assets which increase in value over time, unlike debt for consumables which decrease in value.

- Property Friends usually arranges the purchase of five to 10 house and land packages in an estate at once. This group buying power brings savings to individual investors of thousands of dollars with every transaction.

- Small business people do their best to keep good clients, especially when there is the perceived risk of losing a group of them if they don't. This ensures that Property Friends gain levels of service rarely seen elsewhere.

TEAMWORK MAKES IT EASIER

Helping each other to Win

It is said that TEAM stands for **T**ogether **E**veryone **A**chieves **M**ore. This is as true in the world of property as it is in other endeavors. Let me show you.

When the average buyer purchases a house and land package leveraged in a Self-Managed Superannuation Fund (SMSF), the transaction is about $25,000 more expensive than it needs to be. Why? Because many of the costs are paid twice - once by the builder and a second time by the buyer.

The builder buys the land on which to construct the house. He pays stamp duty. He borrows money for the land and has to pay loan fees, interest and conveyancing charges. And he borrows more money for the materials to build the house, which means he has to increase his profit margin to cover all these costs.

Imagine what would happen if most of these expenses could be paid only once. Think about the possibilities if the land developer and the builder had a business relationship that allowed the builder access to the land without having to pay for it at the beginning.

After four years of hard work and negotiation, Property Friends has developed a system that can streamline the transactional stages of house construction and finance to avoid the double whammy of many costs being paid twice, by two separate people, for essentially the same service.

The result is big savings for everyone, especially property buyers, better cash flow for builders, more sales for land developers and a more efficient system for everyone. This system can be applied only under certain circumstances, but it is worth its weight in gold when the possibility arises.

Refer to the Property Friends DVD <u>Self Managed Super Funds</u> (https://goo.gl/3MFsVv).

After being involved in more than 350 house and land purchases for investors since 2005, Property Friends has seen every aspect of buying investment property first hand many times. We know what works, where savings can be made and how to simplify processes that risk getting projects bogged down.

We have established long-term working relationships with many of the people with whom we do business. We are responsible for clients coming to them, so they look after us in the way that valued clients are respected and consulted.

One of the objectives of Property Friends is for everyone involved in our transactions to benefit from their involvement with us. Indeed, I refer to our way of doing business as a win-win-win-win. The land developer wins because he gains several sales at once.

The builder wins because he can construct several similar houses in the same area at the same time, saving him money through the economy of scale of the work we bring, and the property investor wins because they get the best possible deal which ensures they have made a return on their property by the time the first tenants move in.

Ulla and I win because we earn a fee for service and very often we are part of the team who is buying. On top of that, we all gain new friends in business.

> '**We have established long-term working relationships with many of the people with whom we do business. We are responsible for clients coming to them, so they look after us in the way that valued clients are respected and consulted.**'

Working together

The idea of teamwork is very important to Property Friends. Our principles are based on doing the right thing by the people with whom we do business and treating them as we like to be treated. Obviously, this means being honest and open in communication. All our transactions are transparent.

There are no hidden fees or commissions embedded in any dealings with anyone. Everyone in Property Friends, including Ulla and I, pay the same for any service we gain in buying a property and everything that is involved with that. We believe this gives us strength in the marketplace because we are not bound to deal with any particular company beyond respecting them for reliable, efficient and honest service.

If we get that from our service providers, we stick with them. If not, there is nothing stopping us from taking our business elsewhere, usually to one of their competitors.

By not having any financial ties to anyone, Property Friends has the greatest flexibility to look for and receive the best service.

Investors who buy using the Property Friends system are encouraged to use their own consultants, such as solicitors and finance brokers, but we have established links with all the experts required if investors choose to engage them.

Usually, we contract service providers in bulk. This saves us all money and ensures that the businesses that win our work try hard to give us their best service, so they retain all the Property Friends clients. For example, property managers are diligent in handling our affairs because they know that mistakes could lead to them losing several clients.

Similarly, with things such as depreciation schedules which are required for claiming tax deductions on properties, Property Friends negotiates a price based on the bulk buying power of the group. We often achieve discounts that are the envy of other investors.

Teamwork remains important to Property Friends after an investor has bought a property. We have regular team meetings to keep members up to date with developments in real estate issues, movements in the market and a range of issues as diverse as housing design, new regulations and interest rates.

We call these sessions our "Champion Team" meetings because we believe that everyone there is a champion for having taken action to create wealth for their future and their family. At these events, Property Friends members learn from each other and share their common experiences. They get to know each other and, true to name, some Property Friends become friends in life with each other.

Property Friends also organises regular webinars, newsletters and other educational material to help investors stay on track with their individual investment goals. Beyond organised sessions, members need only to pick up the phone or drop us an email to discuss issues which are important to them.

Success Story

Angela and Nicole

Teamwork pays dividends

The network behind the Property Friends team has been invaluable in helping Angela and Nicole to build their investment portfolio.

Without the referrals to quality professional consultants, Angela and Nicole said their investment journey would have been much more difficult.

"Not only did the numbers add up, but we didn't have to do any of the hard work," Angela said.

"Uwe took the time to help us thoroughly understand every step of the process and he was able to refer us on to professionals such as a solicitor, mortgage broker and rental agent. We found all of these people to be exceptional.

"We would have had to take pot luck if we were left to choose them ourselves. What impressed us most was that these referrals were all selected based on their expertise and experience and not on any kind of referral fee."

Angela and Nicole have bought three properties using Property Friends and found with the first two which have been completed that their equity had grown by more than $40,000 by the time the house was completed.

"We had been looking to invest in residential property for some time but the more we looked and researched, the more overwhelmed we became," Angela said. "We couldn't get the numbers to add up and we were nervous about making a mistake with such a large financial commitment.

"Uwe's knowledge was impressive; his research was thorough, and his investment strategy made sense. What really gave us a level of comfort was knowing that Uwe and Ulla were themselves buying in the same areas that they were recommending to us.

"We didn't have to do any of the hard work. The house plans included everything from curtains and air conditioning to landscaping and fences. We were amazed how every detail had been thought of and included in the price which was far better than anything we could find ourselves," Angela said.

"The all-inclusive deals that Property Friends put together at extraordinary prices mean that it just makes no sense for us to do it ourselves.

"The property looks fantastic, is superbly finished and has everything included. This ensured that we have equity built in from day one and that we were able to lease the property even before handover at above market rent.

"Throughout the building process we received regular updates as well as photos. Uwe and his team were always one step ahead and we felt fully informed at every stage," Angela said.

"You hear that building is a difficult and stressful experience, but this has been smooth sailing from beginning to end.

"Thanks to the professional and efficient work of Property Friends we are well on road to an early and prosperous retirement."

Chapter highlights

- After being involved in more than 350 house and land purchases for investors since 2003, Property Friends has seen every aspect of buying investment property first hand many times. We know what works, where savings can be made and how to simplify processes that risk getting projects bogged down.

- The Property Friends way of doing business is a win-win-win-win which advantages land developers, builders, investors and Property Friends.

- All Property Friends transactions are transparent. There are no hidden fees or commissions embedded in any dealings with anyone. Everyone, including Ulla and I, pay the same for any service.

- We contract service providers in bulk. This saves us all money and ensures that the businesses that win Property Friends work try hard to give us their best service, so they retain all Property Friends clients.

- Teamwork is important to Property Friends after an investor has bought a property. We have regular team meetings to keep members up to date with developments in real estate issues, movements in the market and a range of issues as diverse as housing design, new regulations and interest rates.

USE STRUCTURES TO SAFEGUARD YOUR ASSETS

Safeguard your Assets

Let me give you an example that illustrates how important the right investment structure is.

Before a successful property investor died, he had worked hard to build a portfolio and was comforted by the fact that he had generated enough wealth through his investments for his wife and children to never be stressed about money.

The family was not extremely wealthy but their investments, made strategically and systematically over more than 20 years, created a nest egg that would ease financial pressures on most issues they were likely to face.

Years later, the man's widow remarried a younger man who had his own children. Years after that, she died, leaving the portfolio, now worth considerably more money, in the hands of the second husband.

And that's when the problems started. For all the knowledge, experience and expertise used by the investor in creating his family's wealth he had overlooked one seemingly small but vitally important issue - the structure of his portfolio.

The original investor, being the major breadwinner of the family, bought properties in his own name because his accountant advised that this would give him the greatest tax advantages. But as his portfolio grew, his understanding of structures to protect his assets remained unchanged, and he exposed his family to losing everything he had created.

With the death of the man and then his wife after she remarried, the assets passed to the surviving spouse under the terms of their wills. The children of the original investor were left with nothing.

I am not a solicitor, nor am I licensed to advise anyone on how they should structure their financial affairs, but I have seen enough disastrous examples to know that anyone planning to buy investment property needs to get the right advice to suit their individual circumstances before they commit to a strategy.

There are a multitude of factors to consider when buying an investment, but one that is often overlooked or given limited attention is the structure of the entity under which the property is to be held.

Companies have lower tax rates than the highest personal income tax levels, so does that mean buyers should purchase in the name of a company? The answer differs depending on a number of factors and is not as straightforward as it might appear.

Tax is only one issue to consider. Asset protection is also crucial. What structure will give an investor the greatest ability to retain a property in the event that legal action is taken against them?

If you own more than one property, are they linked through mortgages? If problems were to arise with one, would the others also be exposed to liability?

Trusts are used as a vehicle for maximising asset protection and separating properties from each other. But there are several types of trusts, such as discretionary or family trusts, unit trusts and hybrid trusts, and yet again, they are used for different purposes.

A simple structure which works for many investors - and I am not recommending it because everyone needs to do their own due diligence on what is best for them - is to use a discretionary trust with a company as trustee of the trust. For example, an investor would establish a company with a hypothetical name of XYZ Property Pty Ltd as the trustee of the Surname Family Trust.

Properties can then be bought in the name of the company under the trust structure, which separates the individual investors from the transaction and limits their legal liabilities. It increases the asset protection of the investment and at the same time gives the investors the full benefits of owning the property because they are the beneficiaries of the trust.

> 'After 10 years, the property's value would be expected to have reached more than $800,000, with equity of more than $500,000.'

Self managed superannuation funds

Changes to the law a few years ago allowed self managed superannuation funds (SMSFs) to borrow money to invest in property. But there are very strict rules around how a SMSF can borrow and what it can buy.

Superannuation funds are a great vehicle for property investment for several reasons, one of which is tax. The fund is taxed at a rate of only 15 per cent, far lower than most income tax rates, and capital gains are taxed at the concessional rate of 10 per cent. But that's not all. Once the investor retires and converts earnings in the super fund to a pension, there is no tax on income or capital gains. As a result, an investor who establishes a self-managed super fund and buys property in it while they are working, can gain the benefits of that property tax-free after they retire.

Refer to the Property Friends DVD <u>Self-Managed Super Funds</u> (<u>https://goo.gl/3MFsVv</u>)

It must be emphasised that there are special rules and restrictions governing how a self-managed super fund can deal in property and every investor should seek professional advice before setting up a SMSF as part of their property investment strategy.

I am not licensed to give advice on this subject, but I can tell you how Ulla and I have structured our investments through our self- managed super fund. It should not be read as a recommendation for others, but as an example of how our structure works successfully for us.

We establish a corporate trustee for the SMSF and another corporate trustee for a bare trust which is used to buy and hold each property. A corporate trustee is basically a company that is used as the trustee of an entity.

If we have more than one property, we have a bare trust with its own corporate trustee per property.

When buying house and land packages, our super fund pays for the property once it is fully constructed and ready to rent.

We make no progress payments. Under super fund rules, we are not allowed to personally benefit from use of the residential property. In other words, it must be an investment, not for us to live in.

The purchase contract and the rental management agreement are put in the name of the bare trust and its corporate trustee. That's all that this entity does.

The purchased property is used as security for the bank loan against the property. The bank loans money to the super fund and the super fund makes the loan repayments, receives the rent and pays the property's expenses.

How much the super fund needs to secure a loan for a property obviously depends on the value of the property, but we like to put up between $120,000 and $160,000 for a $400,000 property. Yet when we are doing our cash flow analysis of this property - and any property, for that matter - we calculate that we have put only $1 into the deal.

That way, all the money we have contributed, either up front at the time of purchase or through the loan, is included in our calculations. After all, the equity had to come from somewhere and it cannot be ignored as a free contribution to the property. This way we know that each of our properties is earning its keep and is not being artificially supported by a large lump sum injection at the time of purchase.

Safety in loan structure

Our super fund property loans are of non-recourse, which means that the lender has no ability to claim funds back from us personally, as beneficiaries of the super fund, if the fund is unable to make repayments.

My understanding is that this is the way the Australian Tax Office wants these arrangements to work, to give retirees protection over other assets held by their superannuation funds. Note that very few banks provide true non-recourse lending where the beneficiaries of the underlying trust or directors of the fund are not required to provide a personal guarantee.

So, let's run through a typical example of a property bought through a super fund. This four-bedroom property in Townsville in Queensland, was bought as a new house and land package for $408,000.

At the time of writing, the property is valued at $450,000, an increase of $42,000 in six months or about 10 per cent over that period, which is equal to about 20 per cent a year.

See the property investment analysis data below. This is used purely as an example to illustrate a point. It is not to be taken as financial advice because every investor needs to do their own due diligence according to their individual circumstances.

In this example, there is a contribution of $125,000 at the time of buying, the property is expected to achieve capital growth of 7 per cent a year against inflation of 4 per cent and the interest rate on the loan is of 6.5 per cent a year. We assume a tax rate of 15 per cent in the investor's pre-retirement phase.

Purchase costs totaling $17,455 include stamp duty, conveyancing fees and the Property Friends fee. Other expenses include property management fees, council rates, water charges and loan costs such as application fees, government duties and interest.

Rental income is $450 a week which we calculate for 51 weeks of the year to allow one week of vacancy. Calculations are always done conservatively, whereas some others who want to make their figures look good put in unrealistic figures such as 52 weeks rent.

Before income tax deductions, the property will cost $2144 a year or $41 a week in the first year. But the big benefits come in the non-cash deductions of depreciation on the new buildings and fittings, so that after all tax deductions the property costs $637 a year or $12 a week.

The property becomes cash flow positive in the second year. After five years it is cash flow positive by $31 a week and after 10 years the property is cash flow positive by $100 a week or $5197 a year.

After 10 years, the property's value would be expected to have reached more than $800,000, with equity of more than $500,000.

Property Friends Pty Ltd - Melbourne

PROPERTY INVESTMENT ANALYSIS

Prepared for: 07-Nov-2012
Consultant:
Property: Lot 1080 Fairfield Waters
Description: 400m2 land; 4x2x2 189m2 House by Bentley Builders

---

SUMMARY

Assumptions		Projected results over	10yrs
Property value	$408,000	Property value	$802,598
Initial investment	$125,000	Equity	$501,198
Gross rental yield	5.62%	After tax return/yr	15,46%
Net rental yield	4.28%	Net present value	$235,954
Cap. growth rate	7.00%	**IF SOLD**	
Inflation rate	4.00%	Selling costs & CGT	$57,559
Interest rate	6.50%	Equity	$443,639
Marginal tax rate	15.00%	After tax return/yr	14.13%

COMPUTER PROJECTIONS

Investment Analysis		Projections over 10 years				
End of year	2012	1yr	2yr	3yr	5yr	10yr
Property value	$408,000	436,560	467,119	499,818	572,241	802,598
Purchase costs	$17,455					
Investments	$125,000					
Loan amount	$301,400	301,400	301,400	301,400	301,400	301,400
Equity	$106,600	135,160	165,719	198,418	270,841	501,198
Capital growth rate	7.00%	7.00%	7.00%	7.00%	7.00%	7.00%
Inflation rate (CPI)	4.00%	4.00%	4.00%	4.00%	4.00%	4.00%
Gross rent/week	$450	22,932	23,849	24,803	26,827	32,639
Cash deductions						
Interest (IO)	6.50%	19,591	19,591	19,591	19,591	19,591
Rental expenses	23.44%	5,485	5,704	5,932	6,416	7,806
Pre-tax cash flow	$-125,000	-2,144	-1,446	-720	820	5,242
Non-cash deductions						
Deprec of building	2.50%	4,500	4,500	4,500	4,500	4,500
Deprec of fittings	$20,000	3,208	4,202	2,906	1,496	439
Loan costs	$945	189	189	189	189	
Total deductions		32,973	34,186	33,118	32,192	32,336
Tax credit	15.00%	1,506	1,551	1,247	805	-46
After tax cash flow	$-125,000	-637	105	527	1,625	5,197
Rate of return (IRR)	15.46%	Your cost/(income) per week				
Pre-tax equivalent	18.18%	(12)	(2)	(10)	(31)	(100)

Disclaimer: Note that the computer projections listed above simply illustrate the outcome calculated from the input values and the assumptions contained in the model. Hence the figures can be varied as required and are in no way intended to be a guarantee of future performance. Although the information is provided in good faith, it is also given on the basis that no person using the information, in whole or in part, shall have any claim against Property Friends Pty Ltd - Melbourne.

Success Story

Penny and Scott Hanley

A super way to investment riches

Small business operators Penny and Scott Hanley have taken control of their superannuation fund by buying property to maximise their investment return, tax advantages and asset security.

The couple owned three investment properties and was looking to expand their portfolio but most of their available cash was locked in superannuation. So, they set up a self-managed superannuation fund (SMSF) and bought their fourth property through it.

"It's much better than leaving it sitting there paying tax," Penny said.

"This way we're in control of our super and it's now up to us what happens, not the super fund manager."

Using the super fund to finance the property means that the investment is extremely well protected because the bank has no access to other properties or assets if anything goes wrong.

And once Penny and Scott, from Sydney's Frenchs Forest, retire from their concrete cutting business, income from the super fund will be tax free.

They have used the super fund to buy a new investment property in Townsville through Property Friends, following three similar investments in Queensland and Western Australia outside their super fund with the company.

Chapter highlights

- For all the knowledge, experience and expertise used by some investors in creating their family's wealth, they often overlook one seemingly small but vitally important issue - the structure of their portfolio.

- Changes to the law a few years ago allowed self managed superannuation funds to borrow money to invest in property. But there are very strict rules around how a super fund can borrow and what it can buy.

- An investor who establishes a self managed super fund and buys property in it while they are working can gain the benefits of that property tax-free after they retire.

- How much a super fund needs to secure a loan for a property obviously depends on the value of the property, but we like to put up between $120,000 and $160,000 for a $400,000 property.

MINDSET MATTERS

Plan and take Action

It is a sad truth that many uneducated investors spend more time choosing which type of car they are going to buy than preparing an investment strategy that will determine their financial future for life.

They fail to take a business-like approach to what is very much a business, in every sense of the word. People spend 38 hours a week at work and far less time on planning and managing their investments, so many fall into casual habits when overseeing their property portfolio. This is the biggest mistake they can make.

Controlling property investments does not need to be a full-time job, but it needs to be treated seriously and monitored with diligence, planning and structure.

Owning three investment properties worth $400,000 each is like running a $1.2 million business. And who would operate a business of that size without having robust control mechanisms in place, financial plans, budgets, objectives and incentives driving success?

An old saying that rings true in property investment is: To fail to plan is to plan to fail. But with proper planning, success is very achievable.

Anyone who wants to be a proper investor needs to draw up a budget of their income and expenses and spend at least three months monitoring actual expenses against the draft of expected expenses. Refine and redraw the budget accordingly and continue to adjust it until you know it is accurate and that you are in control of your finances.

Keep re-visiting your budget every quarter to make sure you are still on track. Create a personal profit and loss statement and a balance sheet of assets and liabilities as though you are a business. This is vital. How can you plan to spend on investments if you don't know exactly how much money you have available or what your net worth is?

At the very least save 10 per cent of your income.

Even better, increase this and put aside another 10 per cent for "accumulation or long-term investing", 10 per cent for your financial and property education and 10 per cent for leisure expenses. The last 10 per cent is the money that you can blow frivolously once in a while to reward yourself.

This means you should live off 60 per cent of your income. Ulla and I know from firsthand experience that this structure works very well, not only for people wanting to develop a property portfolio. But we did not invent it. The same message is clear in books which teach similar philosophies such as *The Richest Man in Babylon, Secrets of the Millionaire Mind* and many property investment books.

Educate yourself

At the same time, start your property investment education. Read books and magazines. Attend seminars, study on the internet and talk to people who already invest in property. Find someone successful who you trust and spend time with them. Try to have them mentor you and guide you on your journey of knowledge.

Even better, lock into a network of people that supports and guides your progress with a track record of success and offers assurance that your strategy will work because similar strategies have worked for others and are continuing to bring them rewards. A great way of learning and growing is to be part of a "Mastermind" group, that meets for regular discussions, say, once a week and of course become a member of a team of people that meet regularly to update yourself and hone your skills.

You can request your copy of our DVD *Property Friends Champion Team*.

Endeavour to work out what you like about property investment and what you don't. Focus on key areas such as finance, property types and factors affecting the market and learn about the concepts of capital growth and rental yield and the impact of interest rates and compound interest. Become as knowledgeable as you can so that when you have saved enough money to start investing, you know what you want to invest in.

This is the best recommendation we can give. Save money first, then during the saving period learn the rules of investment, so that once you have enough money to make the investment, your knowledge is sufficient as well.

Once you become an investor you must monitor your investment(s) as though you are the chief executive officer of your new property investment business. Every three months, or at least every six months, do a stock take of your position.

Assess the value of your property against what you owe. How has your net position changed? Do you need to hold your position or has your increased equity given you the option of expanding and buying another property? Even if you decide to do nothing, you will be reassured by the knowledge that your investment is progressing, and you can look forward to improvements in future.

More often than not, property investment is a game against the subconscious mind, since asset growth cannot typically be looked up like you would read a bank statement. Therefore, we have to do our homework to prove to our subconscious that all the effort is worthwhile and that we are advancing financially.

> '**Part of the investor's plan is to look ahead and chart your property investment journey as best as you can as early as possible.**
>
> **This gives your strategy structure, a goal and some measurable milestones which will confirm you are heading in the right direction.**'

Smell the roses

As your investment business develops, remember to reward yourself for goals you have reached. The reward might be nothing more than a night out for dinner or a weekend holiday, but the recognition will work wonders with your subconscious and reaffirm that your investment strategy is on track. You will be able to draw on this confidence when things are slow, or the economy is tough, and you have to ride out a period of slow growth or inactivity.

Sometimes, one partner in a couple who are investors will be driving for expansion and the other will be inclined to take things more slowly.

Being able to see the results of your efforts on the balance sheet or by enjoying a glass of wine watching the sunset together helps to keep your eyes on the ultimate goal of investment leading to more financial options or wealth.

Plan for the worst but expect the best

Part of your business planning needs to include a financial buffer in case things go wrong. And you must develop an exit strategy to cater for the worst-case scenario in the unlikely event that you cannot afford to keep a property, or in case life throws us a "curve ball".

Investors need to be aware that even their most carefully made plans may sometimes not go ahead as scheduled. What happens if someone gets sick and cannot earn an income for a period, loses their job, or if something happens to a member of the family which disrupts your earning capacity?

Insurance for total and permanent disability and life insurance needs to part of an investor's financial plan. This is often covered in superannuation policies. Every investor and their partner need a will and powers of attorney (medical and general) so their affairs can be managed effectively if they die. On top of this, most advisers suggest considering a testamentary trust, for advanced investors.

We recommend a financial buffer of 5 per cent of the purchase price of the property, or $20,000 for a $400,000 purchase. This is to cover six months of living expenses if it is required due to unforeseen circumstances. It does not have to be held as cash in the bank, but it needs to be readily available.

The funds might be able to be redrawn from a loan account or be held in a line of credit against a loan. The main thing to know is that if things don't turn out as you expect, you don't have to use a super expensive credit card just to keep living.

One of the benefits of the Property Friends strategy is that investors generate equity in their properties by buying as a group to save costs and carefully selecting investments to buy under market value. Generally, investors will have "manufactured" equity of at least $25,000 in this way before their first tenants move in. Therefore, investors usually have a financial buffer within 12 months of committing to buy the property.

Nevertheless, investors should plan an exit strategy for their investment before they commit to it. This ensures that no matter what happens, they have a plan to deal with it, even if it is not what you ideally want to do.

If something goes wrong, you can use the funds set aside as a buffer, revalue the property and refinance it using its increased equity or sell it as a last resort. In any event, it is worthwhile having a strategy developed before you ever need to enact it.

Refer to the Property Friends CD Property Strategies Revealed (https://goo.gl/RRmCui)

Identify your goals

Part of the investor's plan is to look ahead and chart your property investment journey as best as you can as early as possible. This gives your strategy structure, a goal and some measurable milestones which will confirm you are heading in the right direction. Ideally, the investor will know how much they want their portfolio to generate for them in passive income by a certain date.

Or they might have a goal of a certain number of properties which they believe will achieve their objective. Or their plan might be to have only one or two properties over the long term. Everyone is different, and many will have varying aspirations and levels of determination and financial ability, but provided the final goal is visualised at the start, you can draw a road map to reach your destination.

For example, do you want to build a portfolio, and if so, how big? Why? What do you want to be able to do with it? Do you require an annual income of a certain amount? How much in net assets do you need to achieve that?

Remember the golden saying - What you can conceive and believe you can achieve!

If you are aiming for a passive annual income of $75,000 in retirement, a basic rule of thumb would suggest you will need net assets of $1.5 million, (i.e. the value of your portfolio must be $1.5 million more than the total loans on the properties) based on the investments generating income or increasing in value by a total of 5 per cent a year.

Depending on the size of your goal, you will have to structure your investments accordingly. Should you buy in the name of the person who earns the highest income to maximise tax deductions? The answer will differ according to how many properties you have and a range of other factors.

As the size of the portfolio grows, so does its complexity. What might be recommended to an investor owning one property might not be the best advice for someone with five.

Protect your assets

Asset protection is an issue that affects decision making and assessment of company and trust structures becomes increasingly important as an investor's portfolio grows. In this regard, each investor needs to gain specialist taxation and legal advice according to their individual needs.

An investor's final goal will also determine which type of properties they buy and when. Some offer more capital growth than rental yield and vice versa. When investors are starting their journey with property they are more inclined to favour capital growth, especially if they are many years from retirement, because this approach can develop the asset base more quickly than focusing on yield.

From there, other properties can be added to the portfolio using equity to drive its expansion, but later, the investor might favour properties offering a strong rental yield because they help pay for the portfolio or lifestyle options that become available after years of investment.

In a nutshell, it's horses for courses. One strategy does not fit all investors. But by educating yourself about the types of strategies in the market and their advantages and disadvantages you can develop a plan that works for you.

We hope that Property Friends can walk beside you along your path to financial success.

Success Story

Neil and Lynn McNabb

Goal setting reaps rewards

Ten years ago, Neil and Lynn McNabb developed a plan for their financial future. It revolved around them buying a group of properties over time that would increase in value to enable them to use the equity to assist their retail business and pay them a passive income along the way.

After buying four investments with the help of Property Friends they achieved their goal - and more. The portfolio building strategy outlined by Property Friends exceeded the McNabb's expectations and gave them more options for the future.

"If I'd devoted more time to it I would probably have been better off scaling down the business and getting more into property," Neil said.

"It's a good avenue for the long-term, provided you've done the research - that's the secret. And you make money when you buy. We've done very well with the deals that Property Friends has put together because they've picked the right locations and the entry prices have been great."

One of the properties in their portfolio increased in value from $300,000 to $550,000 within four years.

The three other Property Friends investments have all achieved solid capital gains which have been invaluable in providing a nest egg for the couple's retirement.

Now semi-retired, they moved to Port Macquarie in NSW a few years ago but continue to operate their Melbourne business with the flexibility of being able to use the value of their investments to fund their golden years.

Chapter highlights

- Controlling property investments does not need to be a full-time job, but it needs to be treated as seriously as though it is and monitored with diligence, planning and structure.

- Remember two old sayings:
  1. To fail to plan is to plan to fail.
  2. What you can conceive and believe you can achieve.

- Save money first, then during the saving period learn the rules of investment, so that once you have enough money to make the investment, your knowledge is sufficient as well.

- Every three months, or at least every six months, do a stock take of your position. Assess the value of your property against what you owe. How has your net position changed?

- As your investment business develops, reward yourself for goals you have reached. This will give you confidence when things are slow, or the economy is tough.

- Part of business planning needs to include a financial buffer in case things go wrong. And develop an exit strategy to cater for the worst-case scenario.

- Part of an investor's plan is to look ahead and chart your property investment journey as best as you can as early as possible. This gives a strategy structure, a goal and some measurable milestones.

- Asset protection and assessment of company and trust structures becomes increasingly important as an investor's portfolio grows.

'Along the way, you will be able to meet some people with common interests, learn from them, maybe teach them a thing or two, and share a journey of discovery.'

RELATIONSHIPS
MAGNIFY RETURNS

Friends kick goals Together

Relationships - they are the backbone of any successful business. Property Friends bases its business on the strength of the working relationships it has first and foremost with its members, but also with builders, developers, property managers and other professionals.

Property Friends works hard to find the best people with whom to work. And once we find excellent professionals we stick with them. We give them more work and in return we get first class service. It improves efficiency and results and ensures that if anything goes wrong, there is a well-connected team on hand to fix it.

This is all part of the win-win-win-win philosophy which is central to the Property Friends way of doing business. The people we work with help us to be successful and vice-versa. We cultivate an environment where it is in the interests of people who work for us, to help us to do well.

For information on Property Friends Champion Team please contact us at: info@propertyfriends.com.au

Property Friends believes that it is the quality of the people behind the product that determine the product's success. And we know after arranging construction of more than 350 investment properties in many parts of Australia that we've fine-tuned a system that works.

We chose house and land packages as the best overall residential property investment because, done using the Property Friends methods, this sector of the market offers the best "bang for your buck". In other words, our properties gain the best balance of capital growth and rental yield with the security of investments in economically diverse areas with minimal risk.

We know all the costs and have a pretty accurate picture of the income a property will produce before we start the buying process. Nothing is left to chance. We have intimate knowledge of the area before we consider buying, and often we pick properties before they are on the market to the public, so we select only the best locations in only the best estates.

Refer to the Property Friends CD Property Strategies Revealed (https://goo.gl/RRmCui).

Why do land developers give us the pick of the crop? Because we have relationships with them. When Property Friends arranges to buy five to 10 properties simultaneously, it does wonders for developers' finance approvals and cash flow.

Property Friends members buy as a group, so we get group discounts on a range of goods and services. Generally, investors gain at least $25,000 in group buying savings and equity between when they agree to buy a property and when the first tenants move in eight to 12 months later.

Some have gained $150,000 in this way. Some of the first Property Friends members are on their way to $1 million in net assets, meaning their properties are worth more than $1 million beyond the total loans on them.

Every investor signs the purchase contract for the house and the construction contract for the house directly with the builder and developer, so while we "group" buy at the same time, no-one shares responsibility for their transaction with anyone else, since we are all individual purchasers.

All Property Friends members pay the same price for the same product or service. Ulla and I currently control a substantial number of properties and we often buy properties alongside groups of members. But we get no special favours and pay the same price for everything as everyone.

Buying investment properties the Property Friends way means that investors gain new properties which tenants love, with no, or minimal maintenance costs, which is what owners love. We focus on high quality houses around median prices, that attract above average rents, producing yields of at least 5 per cent, so that owning the investment becomes as financially manageable as possible.

This method also brings maximum tax and depreciation deductions, which again minimises the financial impact of the investment.

With the leverage that banks afford to property, investors can contribute 5 to 20 per cent of a property's value out of their own pocket and gain 100 per cent of the benefits of owning the property. Some of the earliest Property Friends members are now expanding their portfolios without using any of their own money because the value of the properties is increasing so much that they simply draw on their increased equity to finance all the costs of their next investment.

Over time, their properties will give them lifestyle choices which they could only dream about before they became investors. And their retirement years will be far more carefree in the knowledge that their investments have removed many of the financial hurdles which most retirees face.

For some, the goal of building a healthy portfolio will drive their investment strategy. But for others with more modest ambitions, a couple of properties will help them get ahead and ease their financial burden.

WHAT'S NEXT

There is no right or wrong way to invest in property. If you are interested in building or growing your property portfolio, we would love to help because we know our way works and it has worked for so many others.

At Property Friends we have developed a system that works for all people at all stages of life, regardless of their financial goal or investment outlook. With the group mentoring system that we have established, Ulla and I hope to be able to assist you to reach your objectives, no matter how grand or small they might be.

Along the way, you will be able to meet some people with common interests, learn from them, maybe teach them a thing or two, and share a journey of discovery. And at some point, we hope you, too, will gain Property Friends who are, indeed, regardless of anything to do with property, friends.

Take the next step and contact us today

Safe property Investing
for a Secure Financial Future

Trust - Community - Progress

Tel. 03 9758 5331
info@propertyfriends.com.au
https://www.propertyfriends.com.au

Facebook:
https://www.facebook.com/groups/PropertyFriendsCommunity/
https://www.facebook.com/propertyfriends/

Instagram:
https://www.instagram.com/propertyfriendsau/

www.ingramcontent.com/pod-product-compliance
Lightning Source LLC
Chambersburg PA
CBHW021117210326
41598CB00017B/1482